# NEVER BE AFRAID TO BE YOURSELF

Published in the UK by Scholastic, 2023
1 London Bridge, London, SE1 9BG
Scholastic Ireland, 89E Lagan Road, Dublin Industrial Estate, Glasnevin, Dublin, D11 HPSF

SCHOLASTIC and associated logos are trademarks and/or
registered trademarks of Scholastic Inc.

Text and illustrations © Aoife Dooley, 2023

The right of Aoife Dooley to be identified
as the author and illustrator of this work has been asserted by her under
the Copyright, Designs and Patents Act 1988.

ISBN 978 0702 30738 6

A CIP catalogue record for this book is available from the British Library.

Printed by Bell and Bain Limited, Glasgow
Paper made from wood grown in sustainable forests and other controlled sources.

1 3 5 7 9 10 8 6 4 2

www.scholastic.co.uk

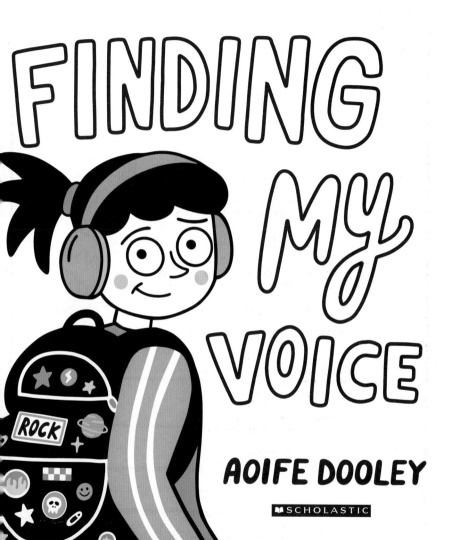

# FINDING MY VOICE

## AOIFE DOOLEY

■SCHOLASTIC

**FRANKIE**

SKETCH PAD

GUITAR MASTER

NAME: FRANKIE

AGE: 12 YEARS OLD

FAVOURITE FOOD: WAFFLES

FAVOURITE MUSIC: ROCK AND POP PUNK

FUN FACT: IS OBSESSED WITH POKÉMON

# CHAPTER 1
## A FRESH START

EPIC GUITAR SOLO

HI, I'M FRANKIE, AND I'M 12 YEARS OLD.

PUNK

AND IN CASE YOU COULDN'T TELL ALREADY...

MUSIC

I LOVE ROCK MUSIC!

THIS SUMMER I LEARNED A LOT ABOUT MYSELF.

I FOUND OUT THAT I'M AUTISTIC FOR ONE!

ME GETTING MY DIAGNOSIS

WHICH IS PRETTY COOL BECAUSE BEFORE THAT, I DIDN'T REALLY UNDERSTAND HOW MY BRAIN WORKED.

AVERAGE BRAIN

AUTISTIC BRAIN

BASICALLY IT MEANS MY BRAIN IS WIRED A BIT DIFFERENTLY TO OTHERS'.

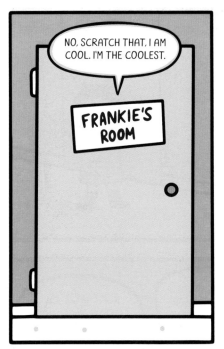

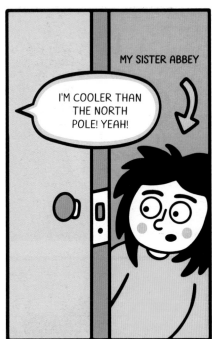

# CHAPTER 2
## NO TALKING!?!

THE NEXT MORNING.

CLINK! CLINK!

BYE MAM!
BYE ABBEY!

ONE THING I'M NOT USED TO IS GETTING THE BUS IN RUSH HOUR TRAFFIC.

TO BE HONEST, I DON'T THINK IT'S SOMETHING I CAN GET USED TO...

← ARMPIT JUICE

IT'S TOO LOUD, TOO SMELLY, TOO STUFFY, TOO PEOPLY.

THIS IS IT, GIRLS! A FRESH START.

WHO KNOWS! WE MIGHT EVEN BE COOL!

YEAH. WE'RE GOING TO BE SO COOL THIS YEAR. I JUST KNOW IT.

EXCEPT THAT'S A LIE. I DON'T KNOW THE FIRST THING ABOUT BEING COOL.

SECONDARY SCHOOL IS WAY BIGGER THAN I THOUGHT.

AND SO ARE THE STUDENTS.

YEAH, SO I DON'T THINK THOSE GROWTH INJECTIONS I GOT IN SPRING WORKED.

AND I THOUGHT I WAS TALL.

WELCOME, EVERYONE! I'M PRINCIPAL KOSLOSKY OR MR KOS FOR SHORT.

I HOPE YOU'RE ALL BRIGHT-EYED AND BUSHY-TAILED!

ANYWAY, LET'S GET STRAIGHT INTO IT, AND START WITH THE SCHOOL RULES!

BLA · BLA
BLA
BLA BLA BLA
BLA
BLA
BLA BLA

I DON'T KNOW WHO THEY WERE TALKING ABOUT, BUT IT MADE ME FEEL BAD.

IS THAT WHAT PEOPLE THINK OF ME? IS THAT WHAT PEOPLE THINK AUTISM IS?!

NO NO NO NO NO! STOP IT, BRAIN! NOT TODAY.

CHAPTER 3
MO AND LISA

FITTING IN IS HARDER THAN I THOUGHT.

HEY! WHAT'S WRONG?

OH, NOTHING.

I CAN ALWAYS TELL WHEN THERE'S SOMETHING WRONG. COME ON! WHAT'S UP?

IT'S JUST TOUGH. WE'RE NOT IN THE SAME CLASSES. I'M TRYING TO MAKE FRIENDS BUT EVERYONE THINKS I'M WEIRD!

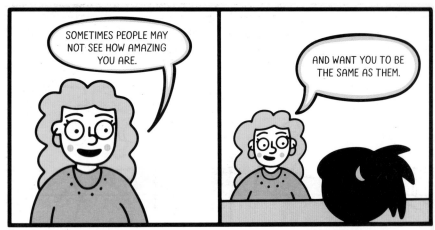

MS POWER IS RIGHT. I JUST NEED TO BE MYSELF.

LUNCH.

HEY GUYS! WHA–

SHE'S HERE! OMG, SHE'S HERE!

LATER IN MUSIC CLASS.

MUSIC ♪
♪ ROOM

THURSDAY

GOOD AFTERNOON, EVERYONE!

WE'RE DOING SOMETHING DIFFERENT TODAY!

EVERYONE GET INTO GROUPS OF TWO!

LIKES PUNK MUSIC

CLASSIC
SKULL BADGE

INTEREST IN
METAL

# CHAPTER 4
## SAM'S MAKEOVER

SAM'S HOUSE.

HEY, SAM, DO YOU THINK NADINE WILL START BULLYING ME AGAIN?

I'M WORRIED THAT SHE'LL TELL EVERYONE THAT I'M AUTISTIC.

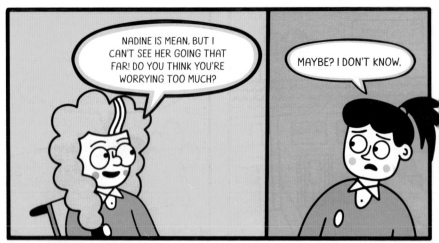

ANYWAY, I'LL BE OUT N A FEW MINUTES! WELL, MAYBE 20.

SAM'S RIGHT. I'M SURE I'M JUST WORRYING FOR NOTHING.

MEANWHILE.

OOOHHH I'M FREAKY FRANKIE AND I HAVE A MILLION FRIENDS.

I'M GOING TO BE THE MOST POPULAR KID AT ST ANTHONY'S. JUST YOU WAIT AND SEE.

OK, IT CAN'T BE THAT HARD! IT'S LIKE DRAWING, BUT ON YOUR FACE.

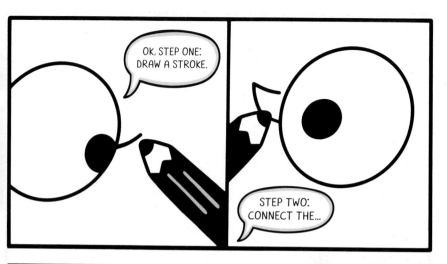

# CHAPTER 5
## GALACTIC TRASH

THE NEXT DAY.

IT'S SATURDAY! YOU KNOW WHAT THAT MEANS!

6:08AM (ALARM)

ONLY 7 HOURS AND 52 MINUTES UNTIL I'M PLAYING WITH A REAL BAND!

ONLY 5 HOURS AND 37 MINUTES!

THE SOLO IS COMING UP.
I'D BETTER DO
SOMETHING MEMORABLE!

GO ONNNN!
HAHA!

WE LOVE YOU, MO!

WE'D GIG IN FRONT OF THOUSANDS. NO, MILLIONS!

AND I'D BE KNOWN AS THE BEAST FROM THE EAST.

# CHAPTER 6
## BITTER SWEET

THE NEXT DAY AT SCHOOL.

SHE'S USUALLY IN BY 8:30 MAX!

MS WIKMAN!

MS WIKMAN.

MS WIKMAN!

BUT NOW I HAVE OTHER THINGS TO WORRY ABOUT.

MY MAM COMPLETELY FLIPPED WHEN SHE SAW IT!

AND I MISS MY RED HAIR. IT WAS ME!

AND ALL FOR NOTHING! THOSE TWO WILL LAUGH AT ME ANYWAY.

YOU'RE IN COUNSELLING? WHAT FOR?

OOOOHHH, PROBABLY SHOULDN'T HAVE SAID THAT...

EMM, JUST FOR SCHOOL STUFF, NOTHING MAJOR.

OH! OK!

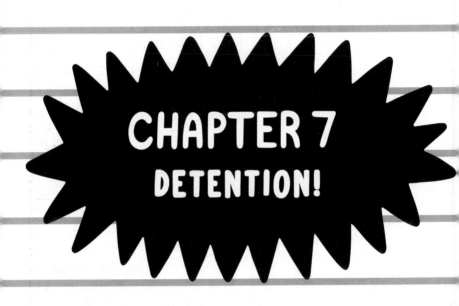

CHAPTER 7
DETENTION!

167

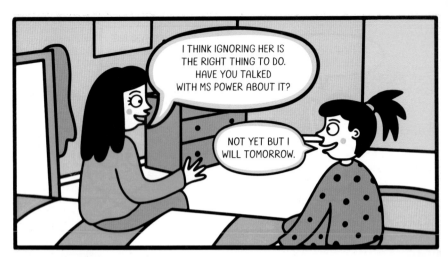

# CHAPTER 8
## HALLOWEEN

HALLOWEEN.

BOO!

CARTOON TIME!

HEY! I WAS WATCHING THAT.

YOU'VE BEEN WATCHING STUFF ALL MORNING.

LOOK WHO JUST GOT HALLOWEEN COSTUMES.

ABBEY, THIS ONE IS YOURS.

AND I GOT THIS ONE FOR YOU, FRANKIE!

THANKS, MAM!

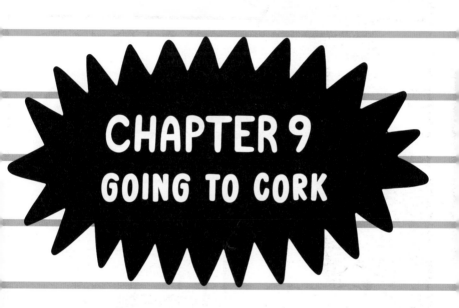

# CHAPTER 9
## GOING TO CORK

I FEEL WAY BETTER THAN I DID A COUPLE OF WEEKS AGO.

WORRYING TOO MUCH ABOUT WHAT PEOPLE THINK

I'M EVEN BACK TO TALKING A BILLION WORDS PER DAY.

IT'S THE FIRST TIME I'VE FELT COMFORTABLE BEING ME.

I'M STILL FINDING MY VOICE AND WHO I AM. THAT MIGHT TAKE ME A WHILE.

LOOKING FOR MY VOICE

I GUESS THIS WILL BE GOOD FOR EXTRA PROOF.

I CAN'T BELIEVE WE SPENT A WHOLE WEEK CLEANING THAT ROOM!

# WHAT'S IN MY BAG

# CHAPTER 10
## BATTLE OF THE BANDS

THE NEXT MORNING.

WAKE UP! RISE AND SHINE, EVERYONE!

TODAY'S THE DAY!

WHAT TIME IS IT?

LATER AT THE MUSIC CLUB.

WE WERE SMASHING THE GIG!
I HOPE REBECCA GOT SOME PHOTOS.

EVERYONE WAS HAVING AN
AMAZING TIME!

WE EVEN HAD SOME
UNLIKELY FANS.

TAP TAP

SOMETIMES IT'S HARD TO BE YOURSELF,
BUT IF YOU TRY YOU MIGHT BE SURPRISED.

# THE END

## (FOR NOW)

**NAME:** SAM

**AGE:** 12 ½ YEARS OLD

**FAVOURITE FOOD:** SPAGHETTI BOLOGNESE

**FAVOURITE MUSIC:** POP PUNK AND POP

**FUN FACT:** LOVES WATCHING NATURE SHOWS

# REBECCA

**AQUARIUS**

HOROSCOPE MAD

COLLECTS RUBBER DUCKS

LOVES CACTI

**NAME:** REBECCA

**AGE:** 13 YEARS OLD

**FAVOURITE FOOD:** BURRITOS

**FAVOURITE MUSIC:** ROCK AND POP

**FUN FACT:** ONCE SAVED AN INJURED SQUIRREL

MO

STEVEN
(AKA STEVIE)

LOVES
TO SING

COOLEST
SHOES

NAME: MO

AGE: 12 YEARS OLD

FAVOURITE FOOD: MAC AND CHEESE

FAVOURITE MUSIC: ROCK AND PUNK

FUN FACT: LOVES HORROR MOVIES

**BIG LISA**

DRUM STICKS

LOVES TO SKATE

COLLECTS KEY RINGS

SPAIN

NAME: LISA

AGE: 12 ¹/₂ YEARS OLD

FAVOURITE FOOD: PIZZA

FAVOURITE MUSIC: HEAVY METAL AND JAZZ

FUN FACT: LOVES BEING SARCASTIC

# WHAT'S YOUR STAGE NAME?

PICK THE MONTH YOU WERE BORN AND THE FIRST LETTER
OF YOUR NAME TO FIND OUT YOUR FUNNY STAGE NAME.

| Month | | Letter | | Letter | |
|---|---|---|---|---|---|
| JAN | GALACTIC | A | ARMPIT | N | BRAIN |
| FEB | METAL | B | BANANAS | O | CATS |
| MAR | STEEL | C | CABBAGES | P | POODLE |
| APR | THE WILD | D | BISCUITS | Q | FOOT |
| MAY | STINKY | E | LEMON | R | WAFFLES |
| JUN | THE TAINTED | F | HORSE | S | APES |
| JUL | THE WEIRD | G | BARNACLE | T | OATS |
| AUG | THE CUDDLY | H | CACTUS | U | BEES |
| SEP | DANGER | I | FARTS | V | LOBSTERS |
| OCT | SNAZZY | J | SQUIRREL | W | BREAD ROLL |
| NOV | GLAM | K | RADIATOR | X | CROWS |
| DEC | THE SCARY | L | SOUP | Y | PIGEONS |
| | | M | EGGS | Z | BEATS |

# ACKNOWLEDGEMENTS

I WOULD LIKE TO THANK MY INCREDIBLE EDITORS YASMIN MORRISSEY AND
SOPHIE CASHELL FOR THEIR PATIENCE AND SUPPORT WHILE WORKING ON
*FINDING MY VOICE*. IT'S BEEN A ROLLER COASTER AND I COULDN'T HAVE DONE
IT WITHOUT YOU BOTH. THANK YOU SO MUCH FOR YOUR INPUT AND FOR
MAKING *FINDING MY VOICE* WHAT IT IS. I WOULD LIKE TO THANK MY AMAZING
AGENT FAITH O'GRADY FOR YOUR CONTINUOUS SUPPORT THROUGHOUT
THIS BOOK AND BEYOND.

TO ALL THE TEAM AT SCHOLASTIC, HARRIET DUNLEA, ANDREW BISCOMB,
RACHEL LAWSON, THANK YOU SO MUCH FOR SUPPORTING ME AND THANK YOU
FOR ALL THE WORK YOU DO TO BRING THIS SERIES TO LIFE.

TO MY NANA, ORLA, AND CALLA – THANK YOU FOR YOUR KINDNESS
AND PATIENCE THROUGHOUT THE YEARS. TO MY PARTNER KARL AND MY
FRIENDS FOR ALL YOUR SUPPORT AND FOR BEING THERE NO
MATTER WHAT, EVEN ON MY BAD DAYS.

TO LIBRARIANS IN THE UK, IRELAND AND ACROSS THE WORLD,
TO BOOKSELLERS, SHOPKEEPERS AND ANYONE WHO HAS SUPPORTED
*FRANKIE'S WORLD* IN THE LAST YEAR. THANK YOU SO MUCH FOR HELPING
GET *FRANKIE'S WORLD* OUT THERE AND IN THE RIGHT HANDS. YOUR SUPPORT
HAS HELPED SO MANY KIDS TO START READING AND I CANNOT
THANK YOU ALL ENOUGH FOR THIS.

TO ANY CHILD OR PARENT WHO HAS MESSAGED ME IN THE LAST YEAR,
THANK YOU FOR THE KIND WORDS AND SUPPORT. IT MEANS THE WORLD TO ME
AND I'M SO HAPPY THAT YOU CAN RELATE TO FRANKIE AND HER FRIENDS.

# ABOUT THE
## ★ AUTHOR ★

AOIFE IS AN AWARD WINNING AUTHOR, ILLUSTRATOR AND COMEDIAN
FROM DUBLIN, IRELAND.

AOIFE OFTEN SHARES HER EXPERIENCES OF BEING DIAGNOSED AS
AUTISTIC AT THE AGE OF 27 AND HOW A DIAGNOSIS
HELPED HER TO TRULY UNDERSTAND HERSELF.